Lion

Pig

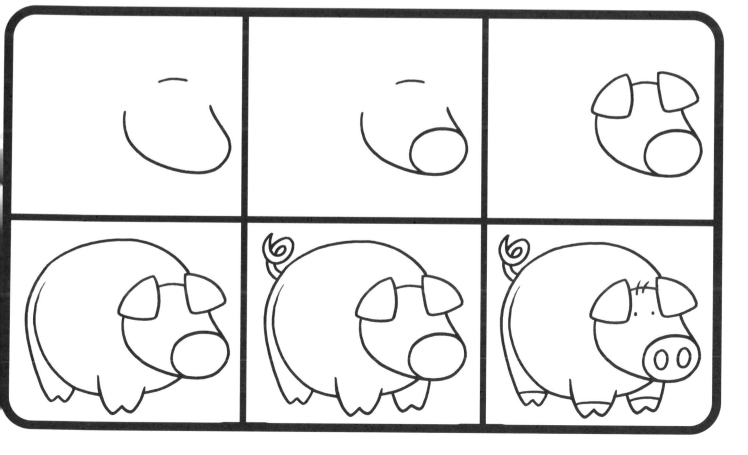

Lobster

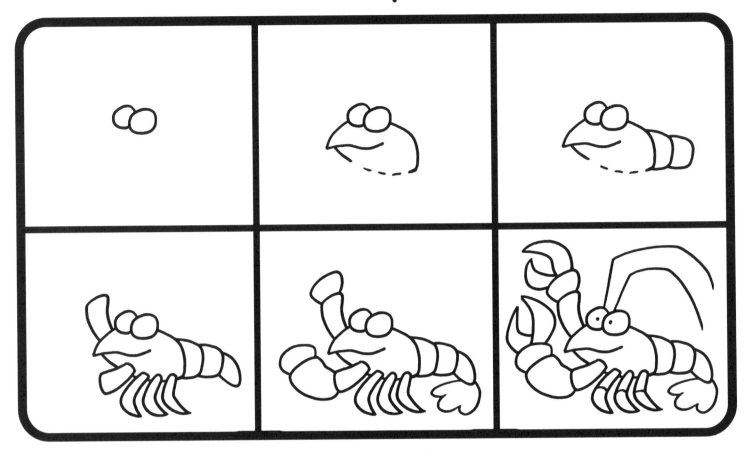

Kangaroo

Eagle

Chimpanzee

cat

Turtle

Dog

Baboon

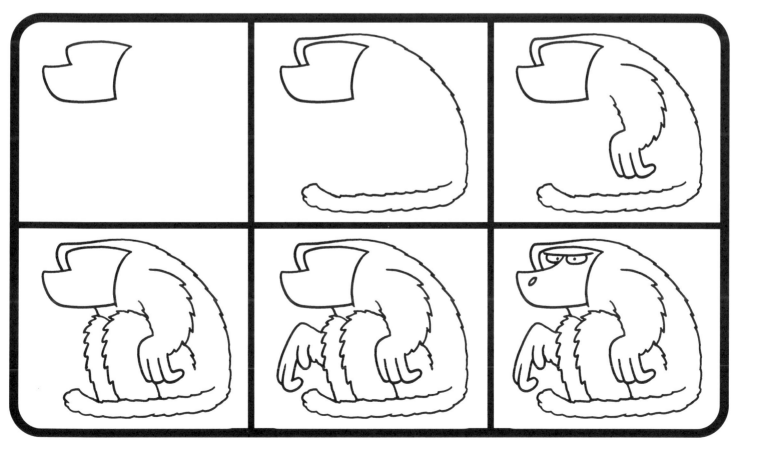

Fish

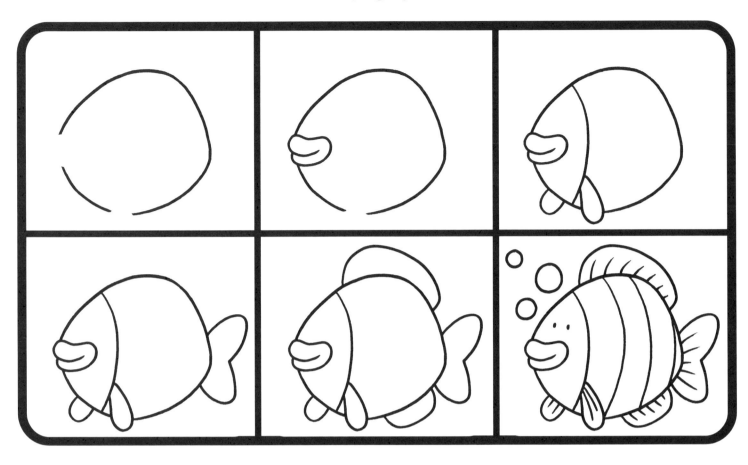

Tiger

Hedgehog

Kiwi

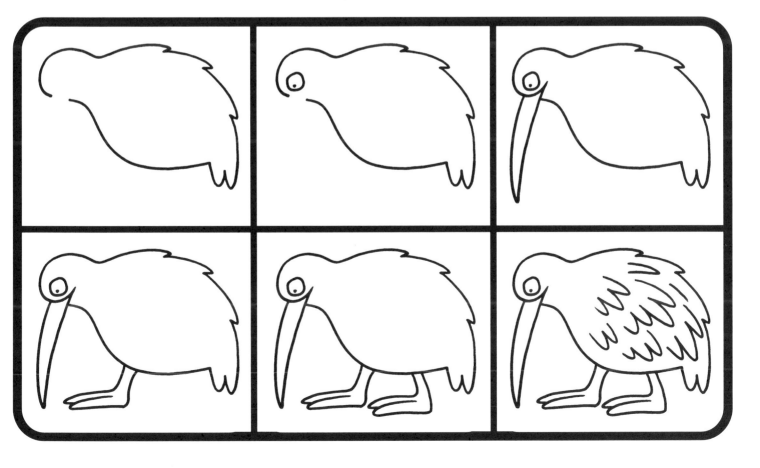

Parrot

Stag Beetle

Anteater

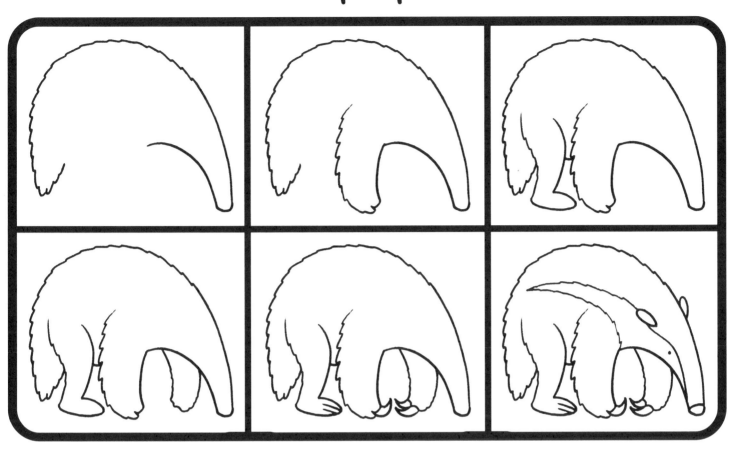

chicken

Budgie

orang-utan

Rhino

Bat

Squirrel

Donkey

Toad

Owl

crab

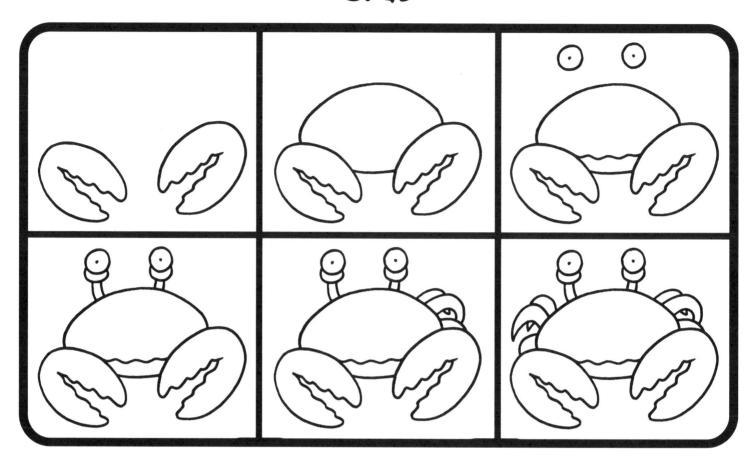

Dolphin

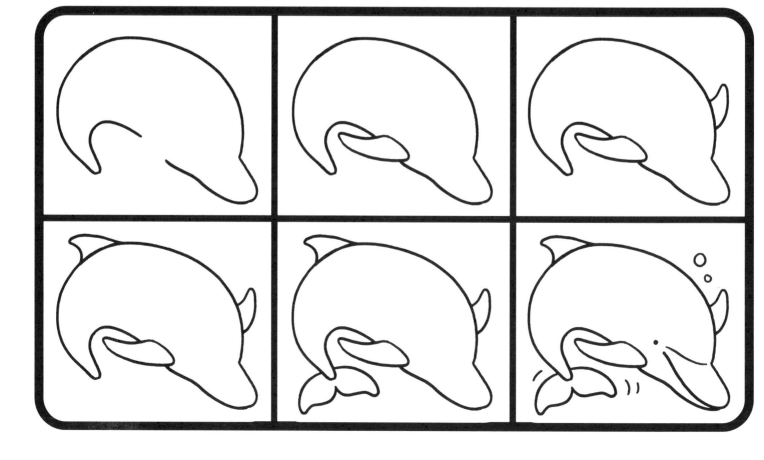

Cow

Rat

Seal

Tortoise

Camel

Ant

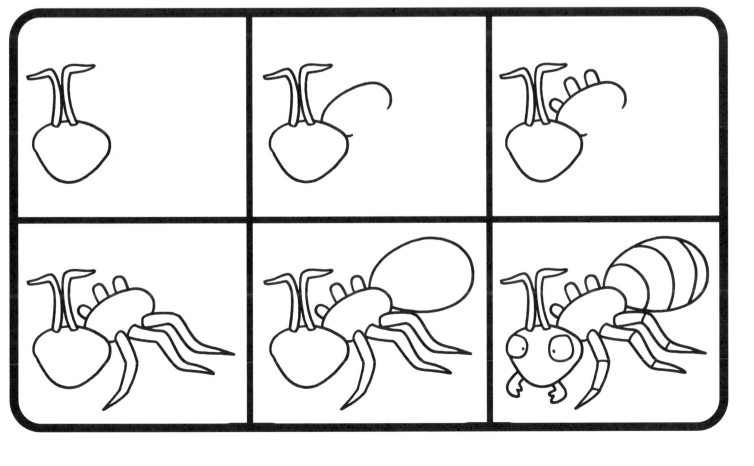

Peacock

Jellyfish

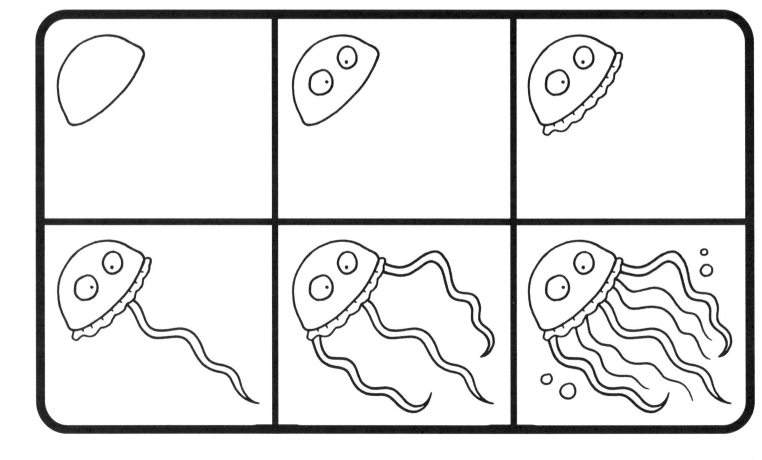

otter

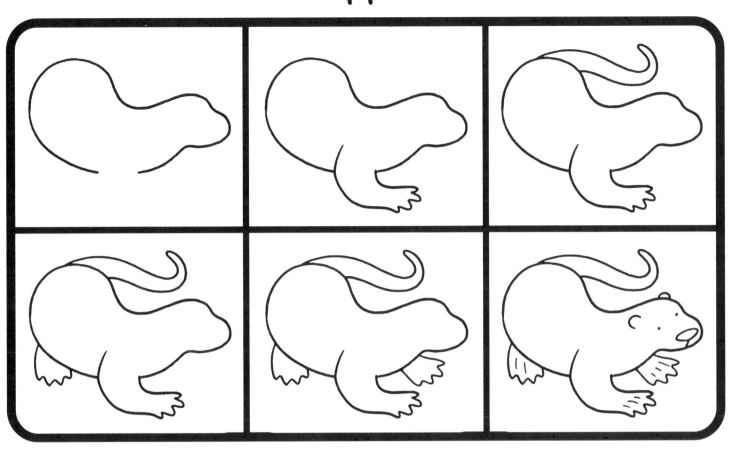

Zebra

Snail

Chameleon

Rabbit

Sheep

Panda

Snake

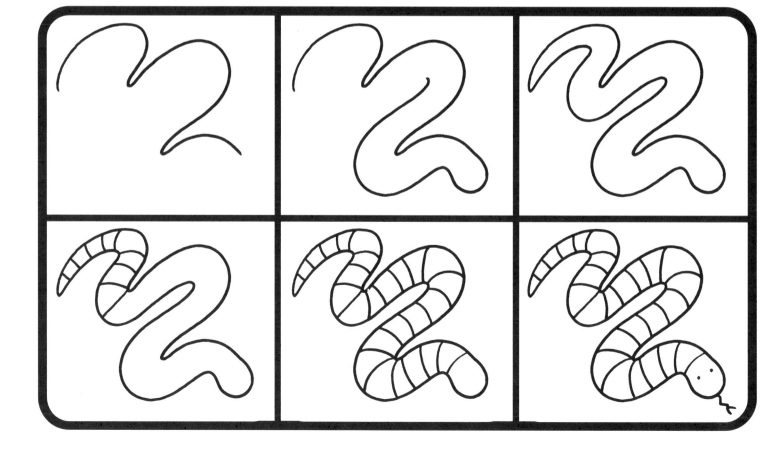

Killer Whale

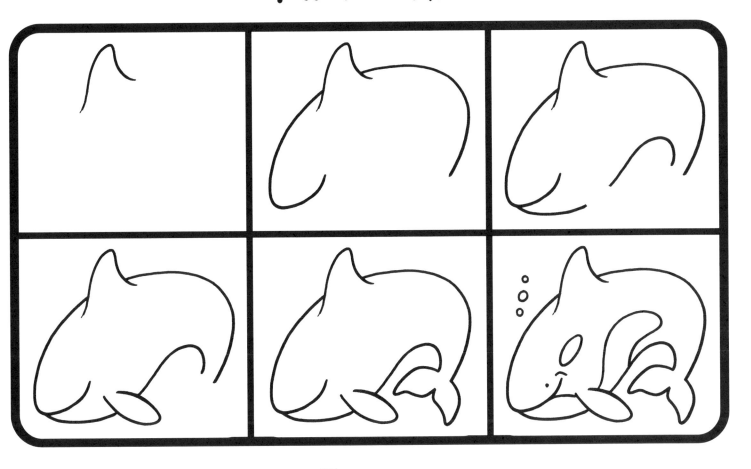

Toucan

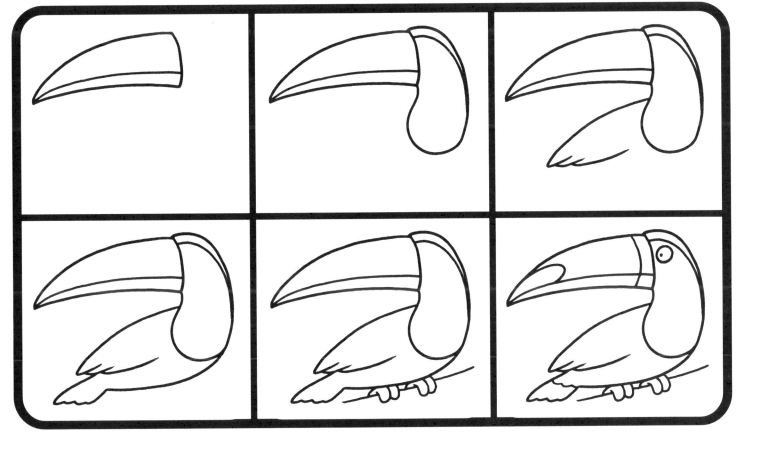

Lemur

Bison

Horse

Penguin

Elephant

Frog

Shark

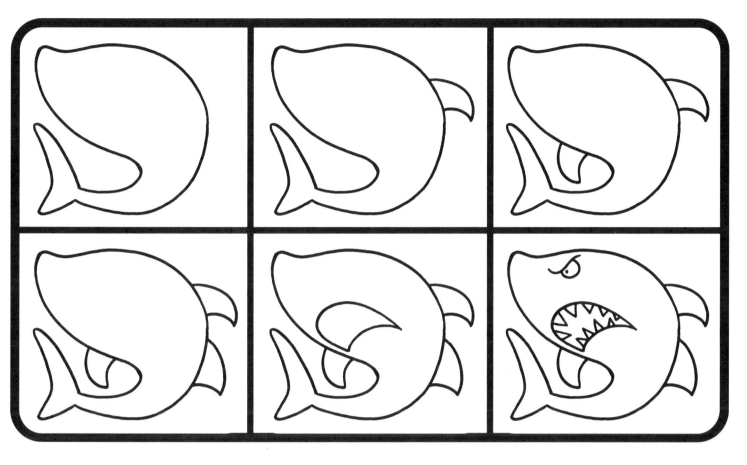

Goat

Panther

Kingfisher

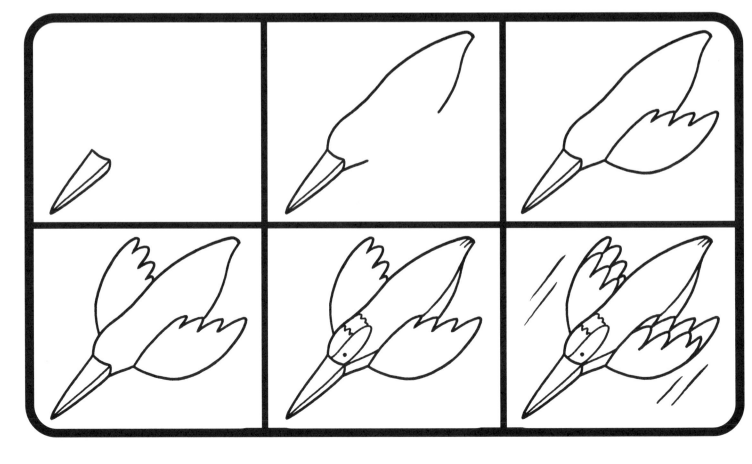

Grasshopper

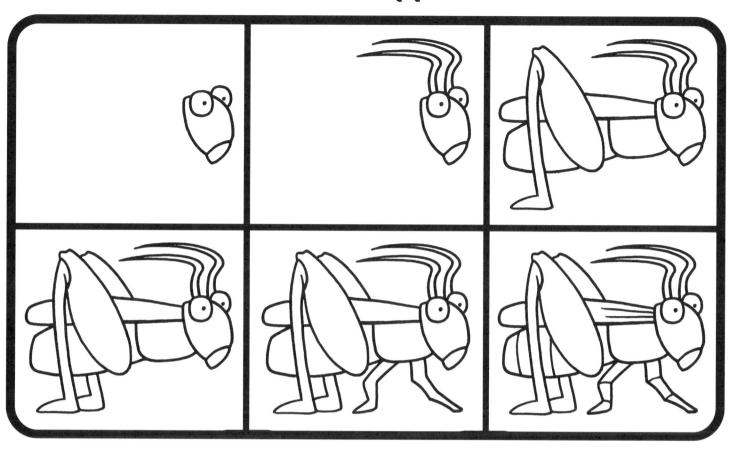

Squid

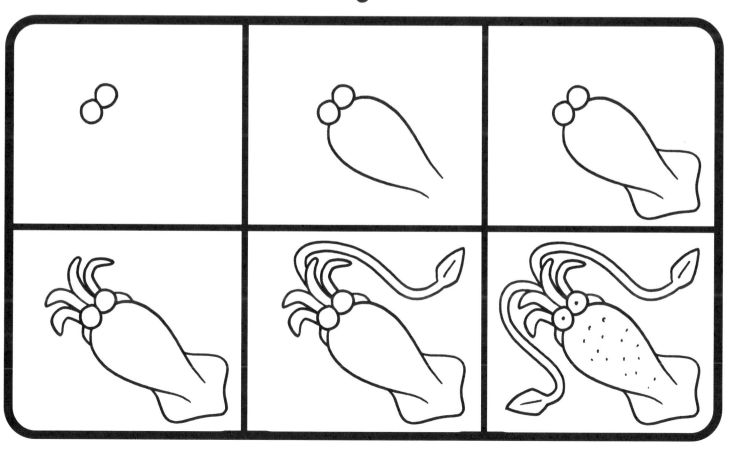

Duck

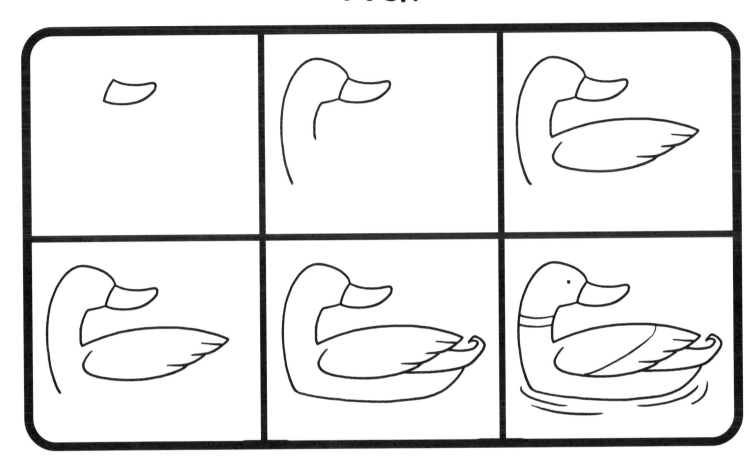

Porcupine

Humpback Whale

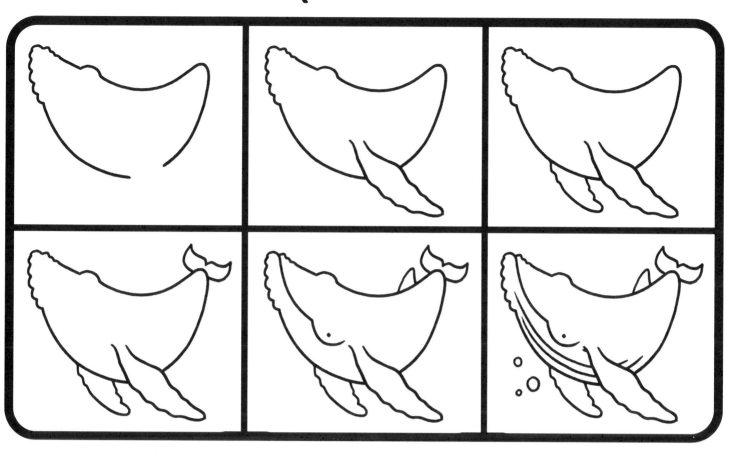

Beaver

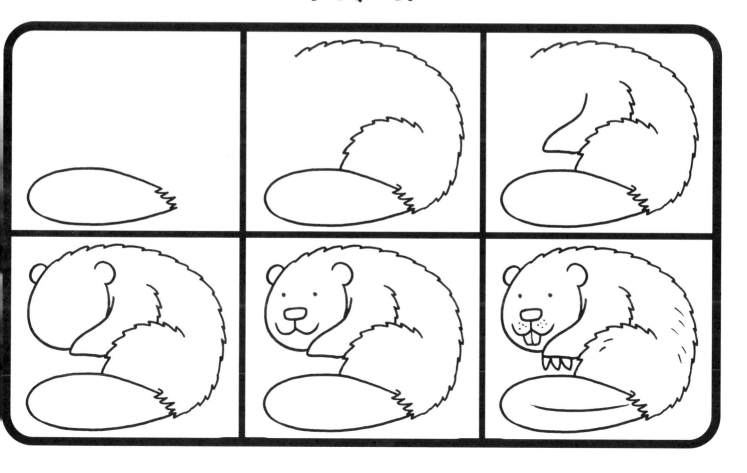

Koala

Walrus

Spider

Mouse

Flamingo

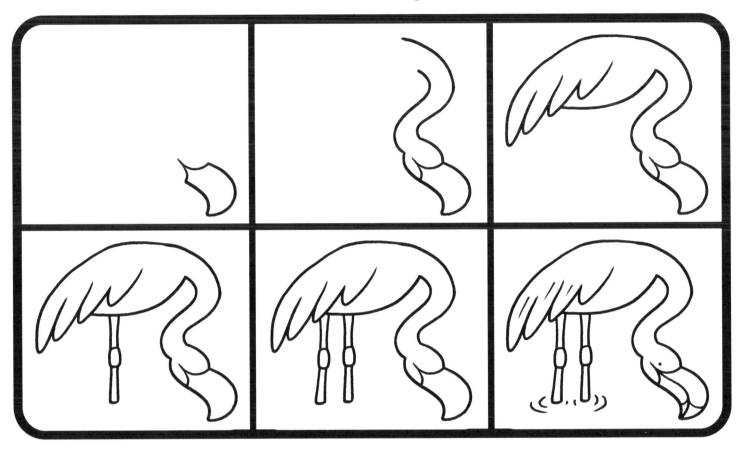

Bear

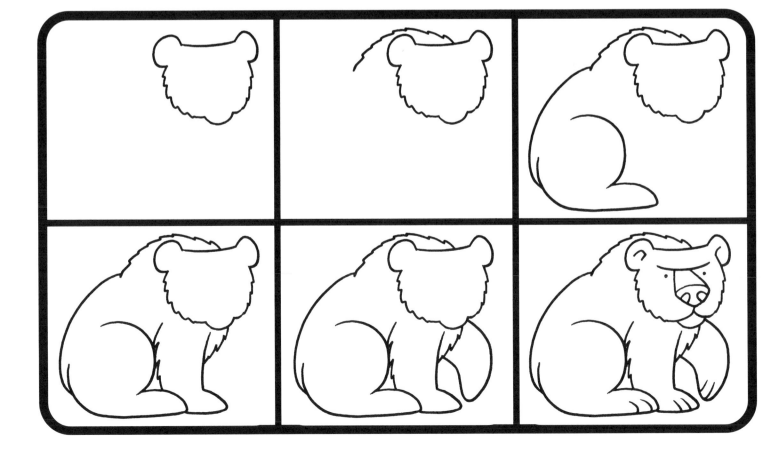

Sloth

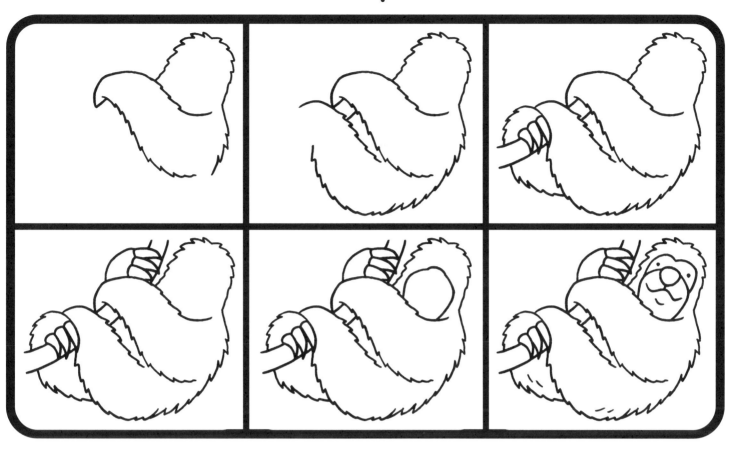

Hippo

Buffalo

Dragonfly

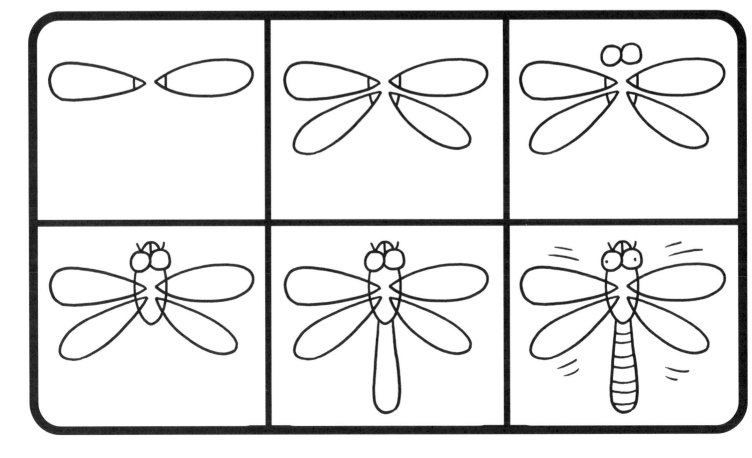

Cheetah

Shrimp

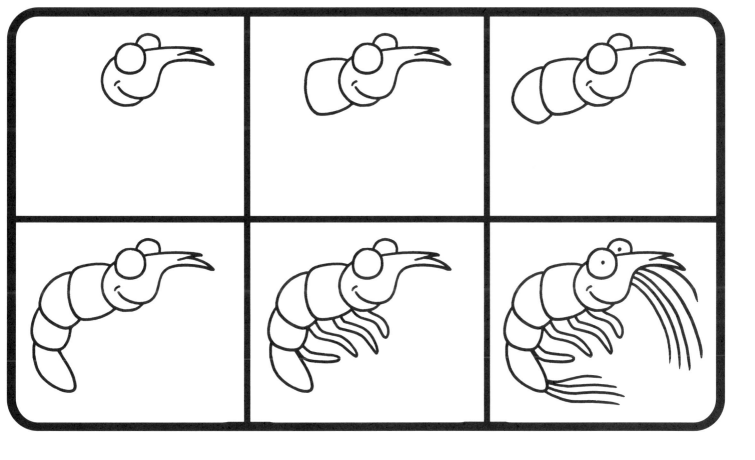

Monkey

Heron

Puffin

Armadillo

Octopus

Bee

ostrich

Gorilla

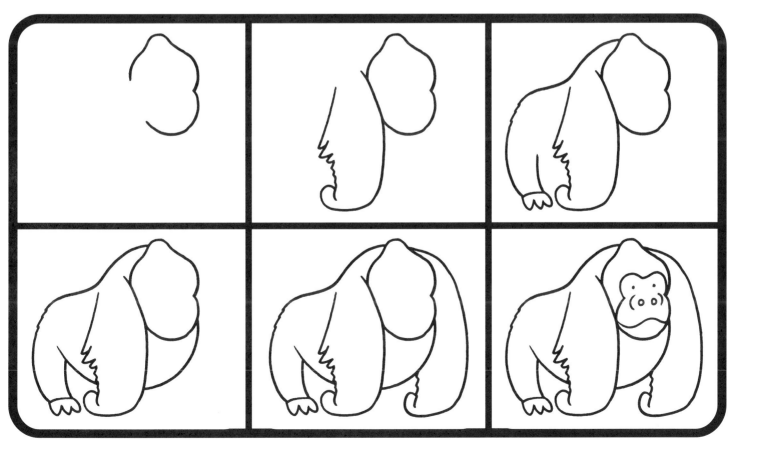

cuttlefish

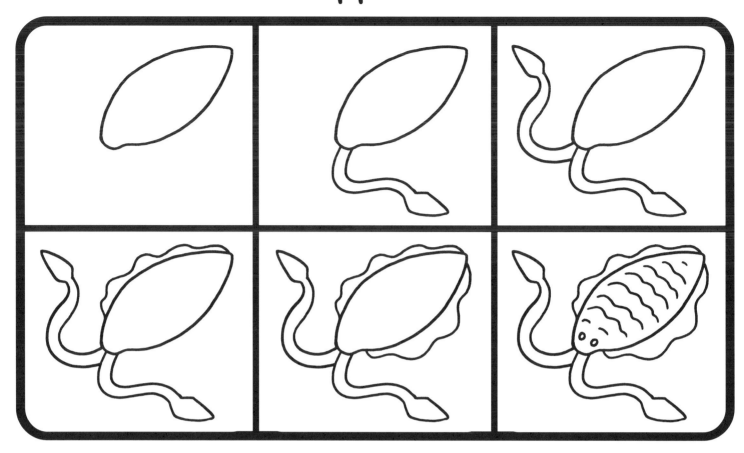

Ladybird

Swan

Manta Ray

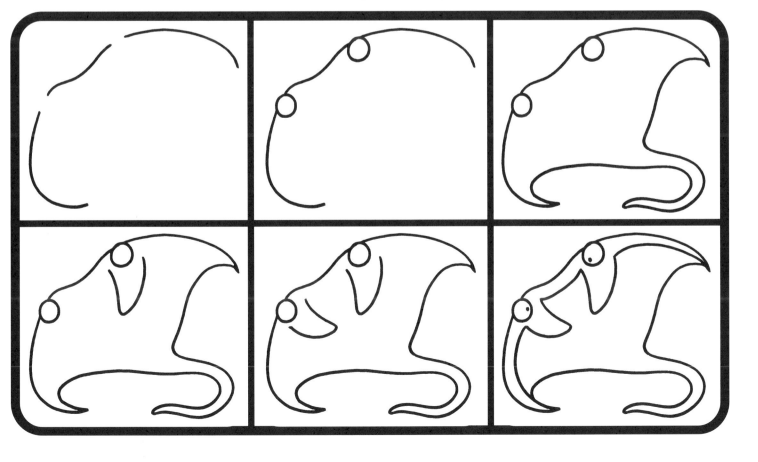

Blue Whale

Crocodile

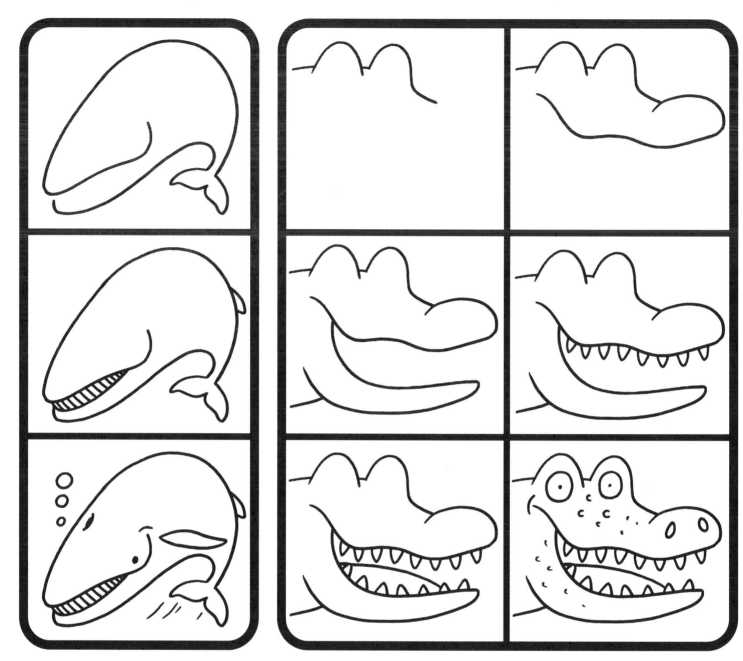

Worm

Wolf

Mole

Angler Fish

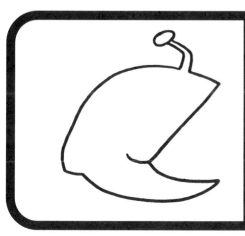

Starfish

Polar Bear

Hammerhead Shark

Housefly

Woodpecker

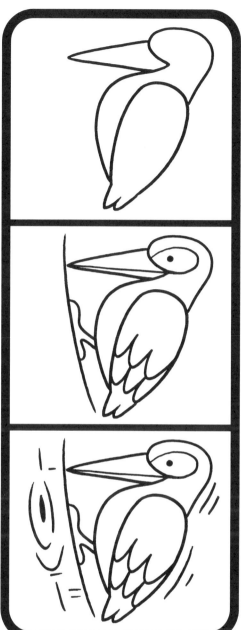

Sperm Whale

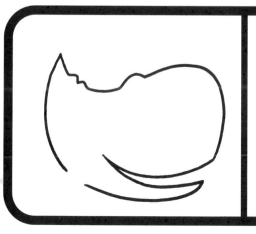

Angel fish

cobra

Butterfly